India For Children

Introduction To India For Kids

By

Shalu Sharma

Disclaimer:

Whilst every care is taken to ensure that the information in this book is as up-to-date and accurate as possible, no responsibility can be taken by the author for any errors or omissions contained herein. Responsibility for any loss, damage, accident or distress resulting from adherence to any advice, suggestions or recommendations is not taken.

Other books by the author:
https://www.amazon.com/author/shalusharma

Hinduism For Kids: Beliefs And Practices
India For Kids: Amazing Facts About India
Religions of the World for Kids
Hindi Language For Kids And Beginners: Speak Hindi Instantly
All about India: Introduction to India for Kids
Mahatma Gandhi For Kids And Beginners
Learn Hindi Numbers: Learning Hindi Numbers 1 to 100
Mother Teresa of Calcutta: Finding God Helping Others: Life of Mother Teresa
Journal for Boys: 101 Thought Provoking Questions
Journal for Girls: 101 Thought Provoking Questions

Table of contents

Introduction to India

India is officially called the Republic of India. It is the seventh largest country in the world found in South Asia. The flag of India is called the Tricolour (or Tricolor).

India lies between the countries of Nepal, China, and Pakistan. Other neighbours of India are Bangladesh, Bhutan, Sri Lanka and Burma (Myanmar).

It is surrounded by large bodies of water on three sides – the Bay of Bengal, the Arabian Sea, and the Indian Ocean. The Himalayas, the highest mountain range in the world, is found on the northern side of the country.

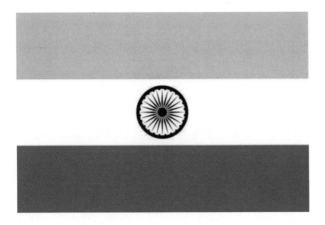

The Indian flag has 3 colors.

India is divided into South India, the Plains or the flat lands (called Indo-Gangetic plains) and the Himalayan Mountains of Northern India. India is so big that it has different climates and environments depending on region.

It has high mountain peaks capped with snow. The powerful winds, lack of oxygen, and the extreme cold in the high mountains do not allow plants to grow. The longest river is the River Indus. The River Ganges is the third largest river in India. People of India consider it a holy river. The wettest place in the world is Mawsynram in North Eastern India.

Indian kids

India also has many tropical rainforests. It has both cold and hot deserts. The Thar Desert is the biggest desert of India. It has fertile plains and uplands.

India is densely populated. After China, India has the largest population in the entire world. It has a population of 1.311 billion. Do you know how many zeros there are in a billion?

New Delhi is the capital of India. Mumbai (or Bombay), Calcutta (or Kolkata), Madras (or Chennai) are other large and well known cities of India.

India has 29 states and 7 union territories that are further divided into smaller districts.

The people of India

People of India are called Indians. In some countries they are referred to as Asians.

Indian people are respectful. They greet each other by placing the palms of their hands together, slightly bowing their heads, and saying "Namaste." Namaste means "I bow to the goodness in you".

A busy street in India.

They regard their elders with even greater respect. Some even touch the feet of older people to express great respect.

The cities of India are a unique blend of the past and the present. The streets are busy. They are packed with modern cars, taxis, and buses, as well as with rickshaws. A rickshaw is an old-fashioned cart that is drawn by a bike or an individual. You also see livestock like cows and camels crowding the streets.

History of India

The inhabitants of India made their home on the Indus River more than 5,000 years ago. They established the cities of Mohenjo Daro and Harappa. They lived in houses made of bricks. They had sewer systems and piped water. For reasons that historians still do not know, the cities were deserted in 1700 B.C.

सत्यमेव जयते

Emblem of India

People from Central Asia arrived in India and made their home there. These were the Aryan people. They spoke and wrote in Sanskrit. Other tribes soon followed and introduced sciences, crafts, and arts.

India was soon invaded by the Mongols who formed the Mughal Empire. During this time, India became the center of great literature, art, and architecture. Many gardens, mosques, roads, and grand tombs, including the world-famous Taj Mahal, were built during this time.

The Europeans arrived in the country and set up trade. Britain soon acquired control over India. The Indians protested against British rule. Led by Mahatma Gandhi, the Indians fought for their independence using nonviolent protests. The British were soon forced to leave India, leaving it as an independent country in the year 1947.

Who was Mahatma Gandhi?

Mohandas Gandhi is one of India's most beloved leaders. He is also called Mahatma Gandhi. Mahatma in Sanskrit means Great Soul, a title that is similar to the Christians' "Saint." The Indians refer to Mahatma as the Father of the Nation. They call him "Bapu" or Father.

Mahatma Gandhi fought for justice. He fought for India's freedom from British rule. He is well-known for teaching the Indians to fight for what is rightfully theirs by using peaceful and non-violent ways.

Mahatma Gandhi is the father of the Nation.

Mahatma was born in India. He was born to a rich family. His father was a respected figure in the community.

Mahatma studied to be a lawyer in the University College in England. After three years, he went back to India and put up his own law office. Unfortunately, his law practice did not do as well as expected.

Mahatma then moved to South Africa to work in one of the law offices there. In South Africa, Mahatma began his work fighting for the civil rights of his fellow Indians.

He went back to India and became a leader in fighting for his country to become independent from the rule of the British Empire.

He taught his countrymen to fight for their rights through non-violent means. He taught them to practice civil disobedience. He taught them to stop working, sit in the streets, and boycott the courts. He taught them to show their protest against British rule through simple non-violent ways. While each protest seemed small on their own, they had a big impact when most of the people in India protested them at the same time.

Mahatma was imprisoned again and again for his role in these protests. While he was in jail, he continued his protest by refusing to eat. The British government became afraid that he would die of starvation. They were afraid about what the Indians would do if this happened. They knew how much the people loved Mahatma. So they released Mahatma from prison.

In 1948, Mahatma was killed while in a prayer meeting. He was killed by a terrorist.

Environment and climate of India

Indian kids having a dip in a pond.

India has a vast, diverse and interesting terrain. It has tropical regions, mountains, hills, and plains. It also has different climates. It enjoys cool, wet, and hot seasons during the year.

The hot season lasts from March to June. Because the country is so large, however, some parts may remain cool during the hot season. The areas found in the mountains usually stay cool even during the official hot season.

The rainy season called "monsoon" is from July to September. During this time, it can be very wet and windy.

India experiences a mild winter during the months of October to February.

Animals of India

India has a variety of animals. It is home to wild animals like the Indian elephant, antelope, tiger and lion. It also has monitor lizards, crocodiles, pythons, and cobras. The animal species in India also include rhinos and river dolphins. You can find bears and rare animals like the snow leopard and black buck in the Himalayan Mountains.

The Indian baby elephant.

It is not unusual to see an elephant ploughing the rice fields in India or carrying heavy or large items for their owners. In some parts of India, you will see use of domesticated elephants in the place of a modern tractors or bulldozers to clear grasslands and forests or to construct buildings.

The people of India look at the monkey as an exceptional animal. Sometimes they are left alone to roam the streets in some parts of India. This is because one of the Gods in India is Hanuman, the monkey God.

The tiger is the national animal of the country. The people of India respect it for its great power and strength, as well as for its beauty, elegance, and grace. One special type of tiger is the Royal Bengal Tiger.

India has many beautiful and multi-colored birds. It is not surprising that many people consider the place a bird watcher's paradise.

The peacock is the country's national bird. It is widely acknowledged for its beauty, as well as for the way it carries itself with great dignity and grace. Many of the folk stories and myths of India have the peacock as one of their characters.

The peacock is seen as a heavenly bird in India.

The people of India show great respect for animals. Many are vegetarians because it is against their religion to kill animals for food. They consider the cow as a sacred animal. If you walk along the streets of India, it is not unusual to see cows wandering along with you and causing traffic to jam. Can you imagine what will happen if you find cows on the streets where you live?

Plants and trees of India

The varied climates of India have also made the country home to a wide variety of plants and flowers. The biggest mangrove forest in the world, the Sundarbans, is found in India. You can see various animals like sharks, dolphins, saltwater crocodiles, and sea turtles swimming in the exact same streams as the tigers.

Lotus is the national flower. This flower grows its roots in the mud. It can grow and re-germinate for several generations. Because of this ability, the people of India see it as a mark of triumph. The beautiful lotus flowers are considered a symbol of a pure mind and heart.

The lotus is the national flower of India.

The banyan tree is India's national tree. You can find a lot of banyan trees across the land. You can find it in many of the villages, temples, and homes in India. It is planted in the roadsides to give shade. In the rural areas, people gather around the banyan tree to meet and hold council. Did you know Buddha found enlightenment while sitting under a banyan tree?

The banyan tree is believed to have cures for many illnesses. The sap is used to heal skin bruises and inflammations. It is also used to treat ulcers, toothaches, and dysentery. An herbal tonic prepared from the seeds and bark of the tree is said to treat fever and diabetes.

The banyan tree also called the "peepal tree". Under this particular banyan tree, Buddha used to sit and meditate.

People consider the tree divine and sacred. It is a symbol of eternal life. It is said to fulfil your wishes. Hindu women have been known to worship the tree and wish for a long successful marriage. In many Hindu myths, the great Lord Shiva is portrayed meditating in deep silence under the tree while his saints gather around his feet.

You can find almost all kinds of plants in India. Tropical trees and palm trees grow abundantly in certain parts of India.

You can also see plants grown commercially. These include coffee, tea, bananas, rubber, pepper, coconut, ginger, citrus fruits, cardamom, and betel nuts. Teak, rosewood, and ironwood flourish in the forests. India is particularly known for its sandalwood, a rare aromatic tree.

Broadleaf trees like the laurel, maple, alder, conifer, and birch are found in the northern region. Dwarf willow, bamboo, and rhododendron are also plentiful. Bamboo and tall grasses grow in the valleys while juniper, fir, and birch are found in the mountain slopes. Farmers cultivate walnut, pear, mango, peach, apricot, and apple trees in the valleys.

Languages and culture of India

India has many languages, dialects, religions, and cultures.

It has more than 1,600 dialects. Eighteen of these languages are recognized as official languages of the country.

Large numbers of people speak Hindi. Many people speak English. These two languages are considered the co-official national languages of the land.

Many signs in Indian are in English.

The Indian people come from varied backgrounds. There are people who have a lot of money. They have big, modern houses with several servants to do the housework. There are also people who are quite poor. Most people belong to the middle class and live in big cities in small homes or apartments or outside the cities in modest homes with backyards and verandas.

Family is considered very important in India. Some still live in large families where you will find grandparents, uncles, aunties, cousins all living in an extended family in one house.

Even today, marriages are arranged by their parents. Indian wedding rituals can be very elaborate and wedding ceremonies can take days.

Religions of India

Religion is an important aspect in India's culture. It is a great influence in the garments, dance, music, and festivities of the country.

Most of the people in India are spiritual. The country does not have an official religion but a majority of its people practice Hinduism. Jainism, Sikhism, and Buddhism are religions that all started in India.

Majority of the people of India are Hindus.

Buddhism is a religion founded by Gautama Buddha, a man born to great riches. It used to be a popular religion in India. It enjoyed the support of the royal courts. But its popularity started to go down until only small pockets of people in India practiced Buddhism. However, it remains to be a major religion in some countries in Asia today.

Majority of Indians believe in Hinduism. A good 80% of India's population is Hindu. Many people also believe in Islam. A smaller number are Buddhists, Sikhs, Christians, Jains, or Parsees.

Ganesha, the elephant God of luck of the Hindus.

Some of the popular Hindu festivals are Diwali (festival of lights), Holi (festival of colors), Durga Puja and birthdays of many Gods and Goddess.

The Taj Mahal

The Taj Mahal is a majestic and beautiful tomb found in Agra, India. It is constructed from white marble stone. Its walls are decorated with many beautiful precious stones and gems.

The Taj Mahal

The Taj Mahal was built during the reign of Emperor Shah Jahan. The emperor had the tomb built to honor his wife, Queen Mumtaj Mahal.

The construction of the building began in 1632. The building was finished in 1653 -- 21 years later. Research shows that 22,000 workmen were assigned to build the Taj Mahal.

Bollywood – Films of India

The people in India love to watch movies. India is known for Bollywood, bit like Hollywood. It is a term coined by Indian media to refer to the Hindi language movies that are produced in India.

People queuing to buy tickets for the movies.

The term is a combination of the words Bombay (where most Hindi language movies are made) and Hollywood (where a majority of American movies are produced).

Many Bollywood movies are also referred to as Masala movies. Masala means spice mixture in Hindi. The term is a reference to how Bollywood movies usually are – a mixture of song and dance routines, romantic comedy or melodrama, and thrilling adventure.

The movies made in India are becoming very popular even in English-speaking countries. Some come with subtitles. Others have English soundtracks aside from the original Hindi language soundtrack.

Bollywood movies are usually musicals. There are many songs and dances in these movies. The movie's soundtrack is usually released to the public before the movie is shown in order to get more people to watch the movie.

Bollywood movies are long. Most take about three hours. A majority of these movies are made with the masses as their target audience.

There are Indian movies that do not follow the Bollywood tradition. They are usually made according to higher standards of quality. However, more people like Bollywood movies more than these more "sophisticated" ones. More people go to the movie houses to watch Bollywood films.

Food of India

There are many types of food in India. It is difficult to describe what the usual "Indian meal" consists of. Most people say that Indian food is spicy. This is true. However, there are other Indian foods that are not spicy. India has desserts that are sweet. It has many types of bread that are simple. There are one-pot dishes that are mild in flavor.

Many Indians prefer to eat vegetables only. Others eat all kinds of food.

Plate of Indian food.

Each region in India has its own specialties. The staple ingredients of one region differ from those of another region. Even the way that a meal is served may differ depending on what particular district in India you visit. Because of these differences, eating Indian food is an exciting experience. Indian food is never boring.

Indians eat food with their hands. However, when they do so, they follow certain basic rules. For example, they should only use their right hand for eating. When they pick up food, they should do so using only the uppermost joints of the fingers. They should not allow their fingers to touch their mouth.

Almost every Indian meal includes flatbread. The Indians use the bread as a spoon to scoop up rice or vegetables. Some even use the flatbread to take their soup although a spoon is usually provided. Some Indians eat meat using a knife and a fork. However, meat is usually served cut into small bite-sized pieces that can easily be eaten with fingers.

The largest meal of the day is usually the one taken at midday. Most Indians prefer to take this meal at home. When they have to eat the midday meal at work, Indians usually bring a prepared meal to work. Sometimes, they order a traditional hot meal from "tiffin." This is what they call a lunch packing service that prepares and delivers meals to the workplace.

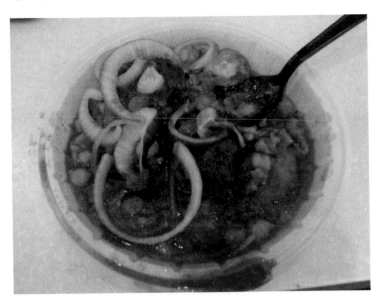

Chaat is a popular Indian snack.

Indians are also fond of taking snacks. There are many different kinds of snacks. Some are salty. Others are sweet or spicy. Sometimes, snack food may be heavy enough to pass off as a light meal. For example, the "pav bhaji" is like a hamburger patty. It is made from a mix of vegetables that are mashed, fried, and put on top of a slice of bread. The "bhel" is another snack highly popular among the people of India. It is made from puffed rice, green peppers, tomato, onions, crunchy chips made from chickpea flour, and tamarind chutney. The pani puri is a small rounded dumpling. Its hollow middle has stuffing made with a combination of chickpea, onion, and potato and a topping of seasoned water. Nuts are roasted and flavored with cumin, paprika, and turmeric. Most of the time, they are topped with a squirt of lemon juice. These snacks are always available from vendors who sell their wares in the streets.

Indians commonly take tea which they call "chai." They put milk and sugar, as well as a blend of spices like cardamom, cinnamon, nutmeg, cloves, and ginger, in their tea. Tea is served with breakfast. It is also served in the late afternoon. It is a very popular refreshment usually served to guests.

"Lassi" is a popular cold drink in India. It is a drink made from buttermilk or yoghurt. It is either served plain or sweetened with mango or rose.

What the people of India wear?

Every state in India has its own particular costume or style. However, there are also certain styles in clothes that are worn across the country.

The usual traditional Indian wear may be made up of a sari worn with a stitched blouse for women. It may also combine either loose pants or a long skirt (ghaghra) and a tunic (salwar kameez).

The salwar kameez is the traditional dress for Indian ladies.

The sari is a traditional costume of India. It is made from cotton or silk. Sometimes, it is made of one solid color; at other times, it may be patterned.

Some saris have detailed embroidery. Others are hand dyed. Some may be decorated with miniature mirrors or metallic designs.

The long sari cloth is wrapped around the waist like a skirt. The remaining cloth is then artfully drawn over the shoulder. The sari is usually partnered with a choli (a stitched form-fitting blouse).

The salwar kameez is another traditional Indian costume. It is a combination of salwar or loose pants and kameez or a long tunic. This outfit can be simple for use at home every day. It can also be decorated handsomely. Like the sari, the salwar kameez is also made from cotton or silk fabric. Indian women usually use an odhni or scarf to complete the outfit.

Colorful sarees

The men in India wear Kurta-Pajama. This attire is a combination of two separate garments. The kurta is a long loose shirt that reaches the knee. The pajama is a drawstring trouser that is made of lightweight material. The Kurta-Pajama can be made from fine rich material like silk or satin and worn for formal gatherings. The Kurta-Pajama made from simple cotton can be used for daily wear, and even as sleepwear.

Men in the villages wear the traditional dhoti which is a cloth tied around the waste extending to the legs.

Basic Hindi words and phrases

Indian kids

Here are some Hindi words and phrases that you might wish to learn.

Hello – Namaste

Goodbye – Alvida

Please – Kripya

I must go – Mujhe jaana hai

Thank you – Dhanyevaad

Friend – Dosth

Tea - Chai

Nice to meet you – Aap se mil ke bahut khusi hui

What's you name – Aap ka naam kya hai

How are you – Aap kaise hai

I am fine – Mai thik hu

What are you doing – Aap kya kaar rahay hai

Where are you going – Aap kaha jaa rahay hau

Pen – Kalam

Books – Kitaab

See you later – Phir milayenge

Thank you

Thank you for buying this book. I hope you have liked it! If you have any questions related to India then feel free to email me on pyt@shalusharma.com.

If you liked this book then please like my Facebook page so that you can keep an eye on new releases: https://www.facebook.com/shalusharmabooks.

If you are thinking of visiting India then you can read travel tips and get more information on my website http://shalusharma.com.

Here are some of my other books that you might wish to consider reading visit http://shalusharma.net.

India For Kids: Amazing Facts About India

Hinduism For Kids: Beliefs And Practices

Religions of the World for Kids

Hindi Language For Kids And Beginners: Speak Hindi Instantly

Hinduism Made Easy: Hindu Religion, Philosophy and Concepts

Mahatma Gandhi For Kids And Beginners

Mother Teresa of Calcutta: Finding God Helping Others: Life of Mother Teresa

Life and Works of Aryabhata

Travel India: Enjoying India to the Fullest: Things to do in India

Facts About Tigers - For Kids

Travel Delhi: Places to Visit in Delhi

Thank you and Namaste

***

Made in the USA
Las Vegas, NV
06 February 2022

43271698R00029